To all the Cheerful Givers

"... for God loveth a cheerful giver."

2 Corinthians 9:7

GROWIN' CHRISTMAS

Karen J. Ashton

Illustrated by
Elspeth C. Young

Based on a True Story

from the life of James A. Jesperson (1914-2005),
a loyal friend and neighbor.

Jim and Petey
were best friends.

They did everything together.

At the age of five, Jim and Petey started school.

The very first day,
Jim and Petey made the
mistake of sharing what
they'd caught that summer.

When Jim lost his first tooth, Petey twisted
and wiggled his tooth for a week until his came out.

When Jim got chicken pox, Petey did too.

When Jim learned to put his hands together
and whistle like a train, Petey did too.

When Jim climbed to the top of a tall cottonwood tree,
Petey did too . . . then he fell out and broke his arm.

Jim and Petey were
always together.
They loved
fishin', swimmin',
shootin' marbles,
chasin' chickens . . .

and findin' constellations in the dark night sky.

They were best buddies,
loyal, true, through and through.

Just before Jim was born, his family fled an attack
by Pancho Villa during the Mexican revolution.

They escaped by hiding in the
last car of the last train
out of Mexico.

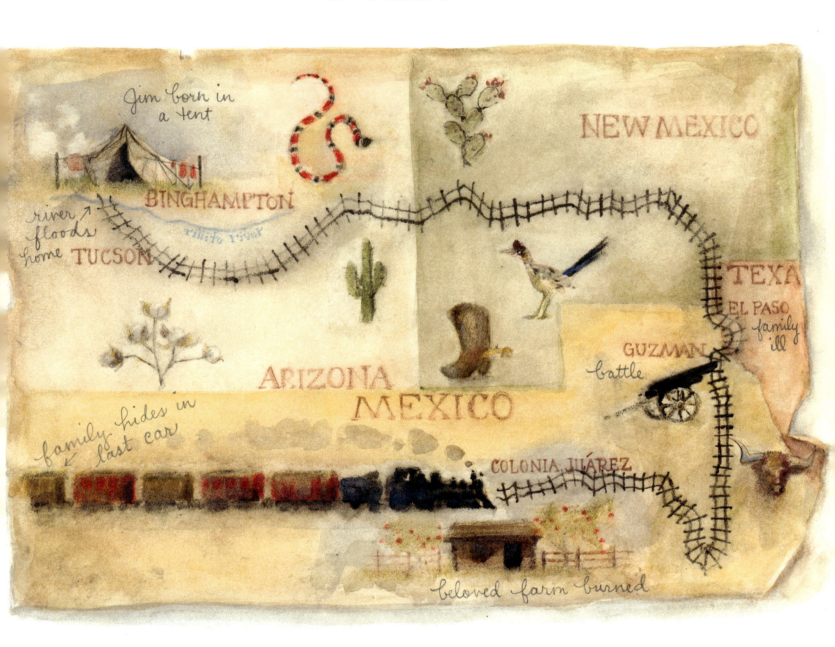

All they had left was each other and hope.

It was enough.

They began to build their lives again in
the hot and dusty Arizona desert,
surrounded by cotton fields
and tumbleweeds.

Jim's dad was a truck farmer . . .

with no truck.

He hauled produce from his small farm to town every week by wagon. His hands were calloused, stained with earth, and cracked from the heat.

He worked from well before the sun came up to long after it went down. By evening he smelled like sweet hay and sweat.

His large and growing
family of one boy
and five girls
was his greatest pride,

and drought was his greatest fear.

Jim's mama made everything

STReTCH

to fit the needs of her family.
She made everything from scratch:
bread, butter, curtains, and clothes.

She made lye soap
so strong it cleaned
the floors,
the laundry,
and almost took
the skin right off
dirty little
children.

Her motto was: "Use it up, wear it out,
make it do, or do without."

Petey's family had their own challenges.

His papa had been sick for as long as Petey could remember. Petey's prayer at the end of each day was that his papa would be better tomorrow.

His house was an old unpainted shack-of-a-thing,
with a hole in the roof and one in the porch as well.
It wasn't much to look at, but it was home to Petey
and he loved it.

Petey's mama sewed, mended,
and laundered other people's clothing.

Everyone in town knew of his family's situation and tried to
help. Even with that, sometimes Petey went to bed hungry.

Early each morning, Petey and Jim
walked the unpaved country road through
town and all the way out to the one-room schoolhouse.

The older boys made them eat dust as they rode by
on their bikes laughing and taunting.

"Hey, you two!
Do you think you'll make it
before teacher rings the bell?"

As Jim and Petey passed the hardware store one day,
they stopped to drool over a
new blue bike standing in the front window.

"Someday, I'm gonna get a bike," said Jim.
"A brand new blue one that's so shiny
you can't stand to look at it when the sun's up!
And when I ride it to school,
everyone will rush out to see it."

"Golly," sighed Petey,
"I ain't never gonna get a bike, Jim.
But I know when you get yours
you'll let me ride on the handlebars,
won't you Jim?
Or double on the back,
and you'll stick your feet out
and I'll put my hands up,
and we'll laugh
all the way to the swimmin' hole!"

Later that evening, Jim said to his dad, "I just *gotta* have a bike! All the big boys have one. Sometimes I want it so bad, it makes my bones ache."

Jim's dad stopped milking and looked up at his son.

"I'm sorry Jim.

I know that kind of ache, but I don't have any money to give you.

I *can* give you land and seed and you can sell what you grow.

We'll make a list of what you'll have to do when I come in tonight."

As they finished the list that evening, Jim's dad asked,

"Are you sure you want to do this, son?"

Jim wasn't sure.

When Jim shared the list with Petey, Petey said, "You can do it, Jim. You can do it! I'll help you. I'll come every day.

And when you get your bike, you'll let me ride on the handlebars, *won't you Jim!*

Or double on the back and you'll stick your feet out and I'll put my hands up, and we'll laugh all the way to the swimmin' hole!"

Petey was as good as his word.
He showed up at Jim's house every day . . .
usually *before* breakfast.

Together, they planned the garden.

They cleared rocks for days.
Jim's dad helped them plow the field.
Jim and Petey set the rows and spread manure from
the barnyard to help things grow.
Then they planted the seeds, and waited.

When the seeds *finally* sprouted, the boys thinned the plants where they grew too close together, watered, pulled the weeds, and battled the bugs that tried to eat their plants.

They watched their garden grow.

When it was blisterin' hot
and the work was grown-man hard, Petey would say,
"We can do it, Jim. We can do it!

And when you get your bike, you'll let me ride on the handlebars, *won't you Jim!* Or double on the back, and you'll stick your feet out and I'll put my hands up . . .

and we'll laugh all the way
to the swimmin' hole!"

When it was harvest time, Jim and Petey spent hours every day picking corn, beets, beans, and cucumbers.

They picked tomatoes, sweet peppers, jalapeños, squash, onions, and watermelon.

They loaded their little wagon, and pulled it door to door selling their produce.

It was bottlin' season and
everyone needed what the boys were sellin'.

Folks were storin' up for hard times, fillin' their cellars
and pantries with jams and jellies, pickles, beets,
beans, corn, tomatoes, and spicy salsa.

One week before Christmas, Jim finally had enough money for his new bike.

Mama took off her old faded house dress, put on her Sunday-go-meetin' dress, and perched her prettiest hat on her head.

Jim's dad hitched the horse to the wagon, and scrubbed his hands with a heavy bristle brush and Mama's strong lye soap.

As Jim sat in the wagon clutchin' his quart jar full of money, he dreamed of bikes—new shiny blue ones.

Jim was so excited! They were going shoppin', shoppin' in town, shoppin' for *his bike!*

The town was decked out
like a Christmas postcard.
When they pulled up in front
of the hardware store,
*the bike had disappeared
from the window!*

It had been replaced by a display of
dolls and tiny tin toys.
Jim's heart stopped.

A small bell jingled as they entered
the hardware store.

"Merry Christmas!" called the clerk from behind the polished wooden counter.

"Did you sell the bike?
The new shiny blue one?"
asked Jim anxiously.
"Well, I've sold many bikes this fall," the clerk laughed,
"but I still have the newest one in town just for you, Jim."

There was a brightly colored banner on the
back wall that read "Secondhand Bicycles."
Jim's eyes scanned the used bikes quickly
and came to rest on the *new* bike standing in front.
There it was: bright, blue, and beautiful.

From behind him, Jim heard his mama gasp.
"Jim! For the price of that bike, you could buy
two used bikes and have money left over."
All Jim's pent-up excitement vanished
like air escaping a balloon.

Jim's dad took Mama by the shoulders and led her away.
"Come on, Mama," he said, "this is Jim's decision."

Jim collapsed onto an old barrel. His mind was spinning. His chest felt like lead. He had known from the beginning that the bike was a terrible extravagance.
But he *really* wanted it!

Jim was numb.

A new idea, faint as a whisper and soft as a breeze floated into his mind. He turned the idea over and over again.

It felt good.
Really good.

It only took Jim a few minutes to make a decision, then a plan.

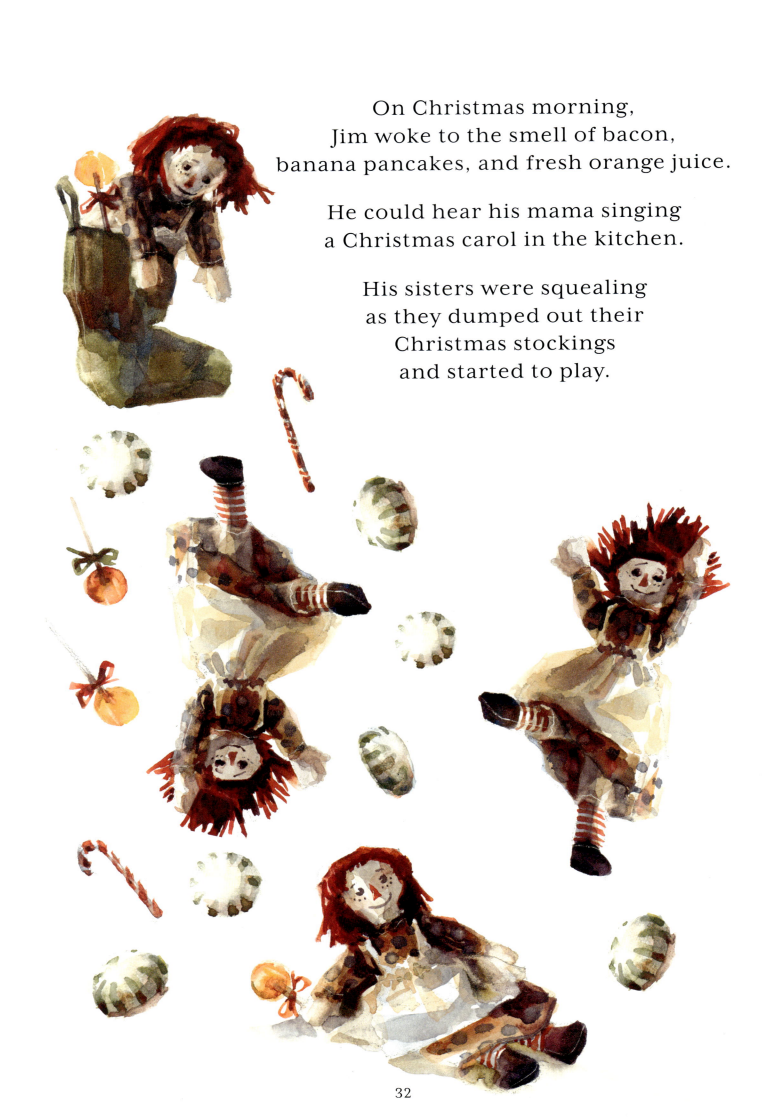

On Christmas morning,
Jim woke to the smell of bacon,
banana pancakes, and fresh orange juice.

He could hear his mama singing
a Christmas carol in the kitchen.

His sisters were squealing
as they dumped out their
Christmas stockings
and started to play.

Jim heard the screen door bang
as his dad returned from milking.

At last, it was time
for Jim's
Christmas plan!

He couldn't wait for breakfast, not for presents,
not for nothin'!

Jim shot out of the house with his dad right behind him.
They collected Jim's surprise from inside the barn
and headed to Petey's house.

Inside Petey's home, Christmas was quieter.
Petey's mama had made cornbread
with honey butter, and the smell filled the tiny home.

Neighbors had dropped off a huge crate filled
with oranges and apples, plus a small brown
paper bag full of hard tack candy.

"I wonder if Jim got his bike," Petey whispered.

Petey's papa felt a catch in his throat.
There hadn't been any presents for Petey that Christmas.

When Jim and his dad
arrived at Petey's house,
Jim's dad hid behind a wild cypress tree.

Jim yelled to Petey from the front yard,
"Merry Christmas, Petey!"

Petey flung the front door open and came racing out.
"Did you get it, Jim? Did you get your bike?"

"I did," said Jim with a smile.

"I got my bike . . .

. . . and I got you one too!"

Petey's smile faded into a question
and then his lower lip began to quiver.

Petey began to cry.

Jim did too.

The End

Acknowledgements

Karen and Elspeth's special thanks belong to the following, without whose kind and capable help, this project would not have been possible.

The descendants of James and Flora Jesperson,
and the family of James A. and Doris Jesperson
Alan Ashton
Rebekah Westfall
Al, Nancy, Tanner, and Ashton Young
Karen Acerson
John C. Maas
Cissy Rasmussen
Annie Ashton
Jim Ekenstam and the staff at North Star Printing
Doug and Lynda Hendrickson of Uppercase Printing, Ink.
Glena Jesperson Wright, Jamie and Eden Rasmussen
Albert C. Young Jr., Sharlie Ann Ferguson, Ruth C. Jarman,
Martha Ann Morris, Ruth M. Cawthorn, and Ruby Cummings

And to our models:
Nathaniel, Dallin, William, and Daven Rasmussen,
Dade, Austin, Kaylee Mae, and Brooklyn Westfall,
James, Janessa, Adeline, Lauren, and Caroline Ashton,
Dana Oldroyd Cusick,
the ladies in Karen's hen house,
and Gus the frog

© 2020 by Karen J. Ashton
All rights reserved
No part of the text may be copied without written consent of
Karen J. Ashton or, in perpetuity, by The Ashton Family Foundation.

Illustrations © 2020 by Elspeth C. Young
All rights reserved
All paintings, drawings, and other pictorial elements are original to this work and are
copyright by Elspeth C. Young. No part of these artworks may be copied in whole or
in part, without written permission from Al Young Studios (https://www.alyoung.com).

Designed by Tanner M. Young

Manufactured in the United States of America

Library of Congress Cataloging-in-Publication Data
Names: Ashton, Karen J. | Young, Elspeth, illustrator.
Title: Growin' Christmas / by Karen J. Ashton ; illustrated by Elspeth C. Young.
Description: Orem, Utah : The Cozy Chair, 2020. | Summary: Two Arizona boys in the 1920s
learn the rewards of hard work and the joy of giving.

Printed in 2020
North Star Printing, 131 West 2050 North, Spanish Fork, Utah 84660-9512
10 9 8 7 6 5 4 3 2 1